This gymnastics goalbook belongs to:

_____

© Dream Co Publishing 2019. ISBN 978-0-9951238-0-9

Sports club bulk orders: orders@dreamcomedia.nz

Contents:

Info	page 1
Level/Badge Achievements	page 2
Encouraging Quotes	page 4
Term Gymnastics Goals	page 6
Weekly Class Goals	page 14

Fun Gymnastics Info:

Name: _____

Age: _____

Recreational level/Class: _____

Club: _____

Coach/es: _____

Favourite skill/s: _____

_____

Favourite apparatus/s: _____

_____

Favourite Olympic gymnast: _____

_____

Favourite gymnastics outfit:_____

Incentive Awards/Badges /Level Achievements

_____

_____

_____

_____

_____

_____

_____

_____

_____

_____

_____

_____

Incentive Awards/Badges /Level Achievements

 *Favourite encouraging words or quotes:*

___

 *You can do it!*

Favourite encouraging words or quotes:

Go for gold!

 My Term Gymnastics Goals:

Date: _____

_____

_____

_____

_____

_____

_____

_____

_____

_____

_____

 Dreams are possible.

My Term Gymnastics Outcomes:

Date: _____

_____

_____

_____

_____

_____

_____

_____

_____

_____

_____

_____

♡ *Flipping out is fun!* ♡

 *My Term Gymnastics Goals:*

Date: _____

_____

_____

_____

_____

_____

_____

_____

_____

_____

_____

 Don't give up!

My Term Gymnastics Outcomes:

Date: _____

_____

_____

_____

_____

_____

_____

_____

_____

_____

_____

 *My Term Gymnastics Goals:*

Date: _____

_____
_____
_____
_____
_____
_____
_____
_____
_____
_____
_____
_____

 Aim high!

My Term Gymnastics Outcomes:

Date: _____

_____
_____
_____
_____
_____
_____
_____
_____
_____
_____
_____

You're a star!

 *My Term Gymnastics Goals:*

Date: _____

_____

_____

_____

_____

_____

_____

_____

_____

_____

If you don't try – you won't know what you're actually capable of.

My Term Gymnastics Outcomes:

Date: _____

_____

_____

_____

_____

_____

_____

_____

_____

_____

_____

_____

♡ *You got this!* ♡

 *My Weekly Class Goals:*

Date: _____

_____

_____

_____

_____

_____

_____

_____

_____

_____

_____

_____

 You're amazing.

My Weekly Class Outcomes:

Date: _____

_____

_____

_____

_____

_____

_____

_____

_____

_____

_____

_____

♡ *Believe – achieve.* ♡

 *My Weekly Class Goals:*

Date: _____

_____

_____

_____

_____

_____

_____

_____

_____

_____

_____

♡ *...it's a gymnast thing.* ♡

My Weekly Class Outcomes:

Date: _____

_____

_____

_____

_____

_____

_____

_____

_____

_____

_____

Be flexible, be strong. And smile!

 *My Weekly Class Goals:*

Date: _____

_____

_____

_____

_____

_____

_____

_____

_____

_____

_____

_____

 You can do it!

My Weekly Class Outcomes:

Date: _____

_____
_____
_____
_____
_____
_____
_____
_____
_____
_____
_____
_____
_____

♡ *Go for gold!* ♡

 *My Weekly Class Goals:*

Date: _____

_____

_____

_____

_____

_____

_____

_____

_____

_____

_____

 Dreams are possible.

My Weekly Class Outcomes:

Date: _____

_____

_____

_____

_____

_____

_____

_____

_____

_____

_____

_____

Flipping out is fun!

 *My Weekly Class Goals:*

Date: _____

_____
_____
_____
_____
_____
_____
_____
_____
_____
_____

 Don't give up!

My Weekly Class Outcomes:

Date: _____

_____

_____

_____

_____

_____

_____

_____

_____

_____

_____

_____

Train like a champion.

 *My Weekly Class Goals:*

Date: _____

_____
_____
_____
_____
_____
_____
_____
_____
_____
_____
_____

 Aim high!

My Weekly Class Outcomes:

Date: _____

_____

_____

_____

_____

_____

_____

_____

_____

_____

_____

_____

♡ *You're a star!* ♡

 *My Weekly Class Goals:*

Date: _____

_____

_____

_____

_____

_____

_____

_____

_____

_____

_____

♡ *Gymnastics counts as flying.* ♡

My Weekly Class Outcomes:

Date: _____

_____

_____

_____

_____

_____

_____

_____

_____

_____

_____

_____

♡ *I love gymnastics!* ♡

 *My Weekly Class Goals:*

Date: _____

_____

_____

_____

_____

_____

_____

_____

_____

_____

_____

 If you don't try – you won't know what you're actually capable of.

My Weekly Class Outcomes:

Date: _____

_____

_____

_____

_____

_____

_____

_____

_____

_____

_____

_____

♡ *You got this!* ♡

 *My Weekly Class Goals:*

Date: _____

_____

_____

_____

_____

_____

_____

_____

_____

_____

_____

Tumbling, leaping, cartwheeling – fun!

My Weekly Class Outcomes:

Date: _____

_____

_____

_____

_____

_____

_____

_____

_____

_____

_____

_____

 Don't forget to have fun.

 *My Weekly Class Goals:*

Date: _____

_____

_____

_____

_____

_____

_____

_____

_____

_____

_____

_____

 Run towards a challenge, not away from it.

My Weekly Class Outcomes:

Date: _____

_____

_____

_____

_____

_____

_____

_____

_____

_____

_____

Standing on your hands is fun.

 *My Weekly Class Goals:*

Date: _____

_____
_____
_____
_____
_____
_____
_____
_____
_____
_____

 You're amazing.

My Weekly Class Outcomes:

Date: _____

_____

_____

_____

_____

_____

_____

_____

_____

_____

_____

♡ *Believe – achieve.* ♡

 *My Weekly Class Goals:*

Date: _____

_____
_____
_____
_____
_____
_____
_____
_____
_____
_____
_____

 ...it's a gymnast thing.

My Weekly Class Outcomes:

Date: _____

_____

_____

_____

_____

_____

_____

_____

_____

_____

_____

_____

♡ *Be flexible, be strong. And smile!* ♡

 *My Weekly Class Goals:*

Date: _____

_____

_____

_____

_____

_____

_____

_____

_____

_____

_____

 You can do it!

My Weekly Class Outcomes:

Date: _____

_____

_____

_____

_____

_____

_____

_____

_____

_____

_____

Go for gold!

 *My Weekly Class Goals:*

Date: _____

_____

_____

_____

_____

_____

_____

_____

_____

_____

_____

 Dreams are possible.

My Weekly Class Outcomes:

Date: _____

_____

_____

_____

_____

_____

_____

_____

_____

_____

_____

_____

♡ *Flipping out is fun!* ♡

 *My Weekly Class Goals:*

Date: _____

_____
_____
_____
_____
_____
_____
_____
_____
_____
_____

My Weekly Class Outcomes:

Date: _____

_____
_____
_____
_____
_____
_____
_____
_____
_____
_____
_____

 Train like a champion.

 *My Weekly Class Goals:*

Date: _____

_____

_____

_____

_____

_____

_____

_____

_____

_____

_____

_____

 Aim high!

My Weekly Class Outcomes:

Date: _____

_____

_____

_____

_____

_____

_____

_____

_____

_____

_____

_____

You're a star!

 *My Weekly Class Goals:*

Date: _____

_____
_____
_____
_____
_____
_____
_____
_____
_____
_____

Gymnastics counts as flying.

My Weekly Class Outcomes:

Date: _____

_____

_____

_____

_____

_____

_____

_____

_____

_____

♡ *I love gymnastics!* ♡

 *My Weekly Class Goals:*

Date: _____

_____
_____
_____
_____
_____
_____
_____
_____
_____
_____

 If you don't try – you won't know what you're actually capable of.

My Weekly Class Outcomes:

Date: _____

_____

_____

_____

_____

_____

_____

_____

_____

_____

_____

_____

_____

You got this!

 *My Weekly Class Goals:*

Date: _____

_____

_____

_____

_____

_____

_____

_____

_____

_____

_____

_____

Tumbling, leaping, cartwheeling – fun!

My Weekly Class Outcomes:

Date: _____

_____

_____

_____

_____

_____

_____

_____

_____

_____

_____

 Don't forget to have fun.

 *My Weekly Class Goals:*

Date: _____

_____

_____

_____

_____

_____

_____

_____

_____

_____

_____

 Run towards a challenge, not away from it.

My Weekly Class Outcomes:

Date: _____

_____

_____

_____

_____

_____

_____

_____

_____

_____

_____

♡ *Standing on your hands is fun.* ♡

 *My Weekly Class Goals:*

Date: _____

_____
_____
_____
_____
_____
_____
_____
_____
_____
_____

♡ *You're amazing.* ♡

My Weekly Class Outcomes:

Date: _____

_____

_____

_____

_____

_____

_____

_____

_____

_____

_____

_____

♡ *Believe – achieve.* ♡

 My Weekly Class Goals:

Date: _____

_____
_____
_____
_____
_____
_____
_____
_____
_____
_____
_____

My Weekly Class Outcomes:

Date: _____

_____

_____

_____

_____

_____

_____

_____

_____

_____

_____

♡ *Be flexible, be strong. And smile!* ♡

 *My Weekly Class Goals:*

Date: _____

_____
_____
_____
_____
_____
_____
_____
_____
_____
_____
_____

You can do it!

My Weekly Class Outcomes:

Date: _____

_____

_____

_____

_____

_____

_____

_____

_____

_____

_____

 Go for gold!

 *My Weekly Class Goals:*

Date: _____

_____

_____

_____

_____

_____

_____

_____

_____

_____

_____

_____

 Dreams are possible.

My Weekly Class Outcomes:

Date: _____

_____

_____

_____

_____

_____

_____

_____

_____

_____

_____

Flipping out is fun!

 *My Weekly Class Goals:*

Date: _____

_____
_____
_____
_____
_____
_____
_____
_____
_____
_____

♡ *Don't give up!* ♡

My Weekly Class Outcomes:

Date: _____

_____

_____

_____

_____

_____

_____

_____

_____

_____

_____

 Train like a champion.

 *My Weekly Class Goals:*

Date: _____

_____

_____

_____

_____

_____

_____

_____

_____

_____

_____

 Gymnastics counts as flying.

My Weekly Class Outcomes:

Date: _____

_____

_____

_____

_____

_____

_____

_____

_____

_____

_____

♡ *I love gymnastics!* ♡

 *My Weekly Class Goals:*

Date: _____

_____

_____

_____

_____

_____

_____

_____

_____

_____

_____

 If you don't try – you won't know what you're actually capable of.

My Weekly Class Outcomes:

Date: _____

_____

_____

_____

_____

_____

_____

_____

_____

_____

_____

_____

♡ *You got this!* ♡

My Weekly Class Goals:

Date: _____

_____
_____
_____
_____
_____
_____
_____
_____
_____
_____

Tumbling, leaping, cartwheeling – fun!

My Weekly Class Outcomes:

Date: _____

_____

_____

_____

_____

_____

_____

_____

_____

_____

_____

♡ *Don't forget to have fun.* ♡

 *My Weekly Class Goals:*

Date: _____

_____

_____

_____

_____

_____

_____

_____

_____

_____

_____

 Run towards a challenge, not away from it.

My Weekly Class Outcomes:

Date: _____

_____

_____

_____

_____

_____

_____

_____

_____

_____

_____

_____

♡ *Standing on your hands is fun.* ♡

 *My Weekly Class Goals:*

Date: _____

_____
_____
_____
_____
_____
_____
_____
_____
_____
_____

 You're amazing.

My Weekly Class Outcomes:

Date: _____

_____

_____

_____

_____

_____

_____

_____

_____

_____

_____

♡ *Believe – achieve.* ♡

 *My Weekly Class Goals:*

Date: _____

_____

_____

_____

_____

_____

_____

_____

_____

_____

_____

♡ ...it's a gymnast thing. ♡

My Weekly Class Outcomes:

Date: _____

_____

_____

_____

_____

_____

_____

_____

_____

_____

_____

Be flexible, be strong. And smile!

 *My Weekly Class Goals:*

Date: _____

_____

_____

_____

_____

_____

_____

_____

_____

_____

_____

♡ *You can do it!* ♡

My Weekly Class Outcomes:

Date: _____

_____

_____

_____

_____

_____

_____

_____

_____

_____

_____

_____

♡ *Go for gold!* ♡

 *My Weekly Class Goals:*

Date: _____

_____
_____
_____
_____
_____
_____
_____
_____
_____
_____
_____

 Dreams are possible.

My Weekly Class Outcomes:

Date: _____

_____

_____

_____

_____

_____

_____

_____

_____

_____

_____

_____

♡ *Flipping out is fun!* ♡

 *My Weekly Class Goals:*

Date: _____

_____
_____
_____
_____
_____
_____
_____
_____
_____
_____
_____

♡ *Don't give up!* ♡

My Weekly Class Outcomes:

Date: _____

_____

_____

_____

_____

_____

_____

_____

_____

_____

_____

_____

♡ *Train like a champion.* ♡

 *My Weekly Class Goals:*

Date: _____

_____

_____

_____

_____

_____

_____

_____

_____

_____

_____

 Aim high!

My Weekly Class Outcomes:

Date: _____

_____

_____

_____

_____

_____

_____

_____

_____

_____

_____

_____

♡ *You're a star!* ♡

 *My Weekly Class Goals:*

Date: _____

_____
_____
_____
_____
_____
_____
_____
_____
_____
_____
_____

 Gymnastics counts as flying.

My Weekly Class Outcomes:

Date: _____

_____

_____

_____

_____

_____

_____

_____

_____

_____

_____

♡ *I love gymnastics!* ♡

 *My Weekly Class Goals:*

Date: _____

_____

_____

_____

_____

_____

_____

_____

_____

_____

 If you don't try – you won't know what you're actually capable of.

My Weekly Class Outcomes:

Date: _____

_____

_____

_____

_____

_____

_____

_____

_____

_____

_____

♡ *You got this!* ♡

 *My Weekly Class Goals:*

Date: _____

_____

_____

_____

_____

_____

_____

_____

_____

_____

_____

 Aim high!

My Weekly Class Outcomes:

Date: _____

_____

_____

_____

_____

_____

_____

_____

_____

_____

_____

♡ *You're a star!* ♡

 *My Weekly Class Goals:*

Date: _____

_____
_____
_____
_____
_____
_____
_____
_____
_____
_____

 Gymnastics counts as flying.

My Weekly Class Outcomes:

Date: _____

_____

_____

_____

_____

_____

_____

_____

_____

_____

_____

_____

♡ *I love gymnastics!* ♡

 My Weekly Class Goals:

Date: _____

_____

_____

_____

_____

_____

_____

_____

_____

_____

_____

 Tumbling, leaping, cartwheeling – fun!

My Weekly Class Outcomes:

Date: _____

_____

_____

_____

_____

_____

_____

_____

_____

_____

_____

♡ *Don't forget to have fun.* ♡

My Weekly Class Goals:

Date: _____

_____

_____

_____

_____

_____

_____

_____

_____

_____

_____

 Run towards a challenge, not away from it.

My Weekly Class Outcomes:

Date: _____

_____

_____

_____

_____

_____

_____

_____

_____

_____

_____

♡ *Standing on your hands is fun.* ♡

Fun space for drawing:

www.ingramcontent.com/pod-product-compliance
Lightning Source LLC
Chambersburg PA
CBHW070436010526
44118CB00014B/2062